The $200 Computer Coupon

Raymond J. McKinley IV

The $200 Computer Coupon

ISBN:
ISBN-13: 978-1468115116

Preface

Hello and thank you for purchasing this book. My name is Raymond J. McKinley IV and I've been in the technology business for over 15 years with titles ranging from PC Tech to Chief Information Systems Engineer. I'm writing this book mainly because I often get asked the question, "I need to buy a new computer. They have one on sale at _____. Can you look at this ad and tell me if it's a good one to buy?". Often, people want a short answer, but to be of any real value to them, the answer tends to be a bit longer. The fact is, most computers are so far ahead of what was out there 5 years ago, that any purchase would be a major upgrade. The problem is, many people don't understand what kind of user they are and why having that understanding will save them money – both now and down the road. By working in the technology field, I was able to observe the benefits and disasters that come from matching (or mismatching) users to computers. Over the years I created a system to help myself better match people to technology. This was initially for business needs, so I created one for the normal consumer allowing me to help others more efficiently.

I would like to take the time to thank a few people. You see, I'm not a writer – not even close, but I have had the privilege of being exposed to some great people in my life. They, along with countless others, convinced me to go beyond my normal self-imposed boundaries and put my thoughts into writing.

To write this book, took effort, belief in myself, encouragement, and a big push. With that said, I would like to first thank Todd Tyler for his leadership and resolute practice of "leading by example". He has showed me what true effort can achieve. He has demonstrated drive, commitment, and principle in ways that have left me with an inventory of fewer excuses and more controls in my path for life. Had I never met him, I may not have begun this book, and most certainly would not have finished it. He has been my best mentor and sincere friend. Second, is my mother, Betty McKinley, who has always believed more in me than I have in myself. She gave me the will to believe in myself. She convinced me that I do have knowledge that others could benefit from knowing. Third I need to thank my father and my son, Raymond J. McKinley the third and fifth. They have been my greatest fans, encouraging me all the way. Next, I would like to thank Cindy Vest for introducing me to Amazon's Kindle Direct Publishing program that has made this book possible. And last, I must acknowledge to the world that my big sister, Belinda Taylor, has pushed me for years (literally) to write this book. Although I hate to admit it, she has been the catalyst of every great thing I've achieved and without a doubt, the biggest pain in my butt. That's why I love her so much.

The $200 Computer Coupon

Table of Contents

Introduction

What is this book about?

This book is simply named The $200 Computer Coupon because learning how to pick your next computer wisely can save at least $200 while getting you what you really want. With understanding this book you should be able to save yourself at least $200 on your next computer purchase.

This is done by teaching you to understand:

1) Who you are as a computer user.

2) What types of computers are out there to choose from?

3) Learning a few basics on how computers are sold.

4) Giving you the tools you need to find what you really want.

Please understand that this book is NOT about finding the cheapest price for a computer. To do that, you can easily do a search for computers on the web or look at the Sunday paper and take your pick. Computers are just like everything else – "You get what you pay for". The $200 Computer

Coupon is more about finding the true bottom line price to what you need in a COMPLETE computing system, and trimming that bottom line down with a plan. This book is the first and biggest step in having that plan. All too often, we find ourselves being nickel and dimed to death by those who, with the best intentions, give flawed advice. My hope is that by the end of this book you will be able to purchase your next computer with confidence as to what you're getting and know that every dime (saved and spent) was worth it.

Who is this book for?

This book is for the everyday Joes, not in the information tech field, that want the biggest bang for the buck – Plain and simple! I made the point of writing this book as if I was informing my mother, or a close friend, on what to buy and why. The WHY is what this book is about, and why you should want to read it. If you enjoy impulse buying, then this book may not be for you. If you don't care about the money you'll save down the road and only want the cheapest item you can find, then this may not be for you. The ideal person for this book is the person (like my Mom) that does not want to hear that it will cost more money to do what they need to do, on the computer they just bought. The $200 Computer Coupon is for those (like my close friend) that want to see the "Bottom Line" and want that Bottom Line to be accurate. This book is for everyone, so that all of us can buy the right technology the first time.

Get to the point!

So, let's get to the point. Getting a great deal on a new desktop is actually a loss of money, if your lifestyle is more suited for a Nettop. Never heard of a Nettop? Then you need to read this book. In today's technology, there are many different types of computers/computing devices out there, and knowing what they are, what they can and can't do, and how your needs fit into what's out there, will save you money – lots of money.

I've broken this book down into four parts; the first part (and the most important) is learning what kind of computer user you are. This is vital to making the best choice on a computer and goes a bit deeper than just saying "OH, I just want to be able to check my email". If checking email is your goal, buy a Smartphone (My job is done… I just saved you the $200 I promised). The second part helps you understand the various types of computers; the major components to know about; and what's current. This goes to the issue of buying a computer that's already out dated by the time you get home. It really does happen! The third part looks at how and where computers are sold, along with their advantages and disadvantages. This is the part that cut's the bottom line down after you know what you really need. The fourth part gives you some tools to use when purchasing your next computer. This will save you time and make you're searching more productive.

What Kind of Computer User are You?

I break computer users into five main categories: Social, Gaming, Business, Students, and Entertainment. Many of us are a blend of two or more categories and we will address this later. For now, understanding these five types is important to knowing who you are as a user.

There are 5 different kinds of users:

- Social
- Gaming
- SOHO
- Students
- Entertainment (Couchers)

The Social User

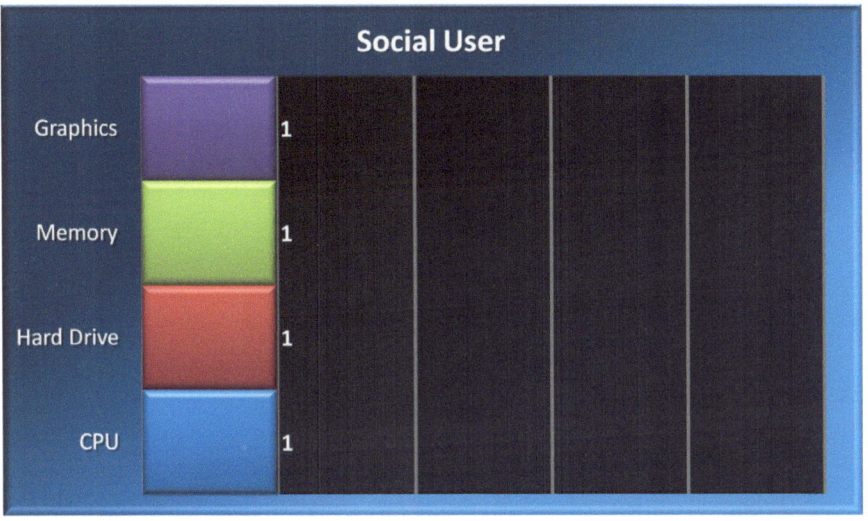

The social user is the most common type of user. Almost everyone falls into this category in some limited form. Social users are more into utilizing computers to socialize using various forms of communication. Don't think on a limited level. People out there including members of your own family are using computers to speak and see each other in real time with a very high level of quality. This category includes things like email, video chat (e.g. Skype), social networking (e.g. Facebook), blogs, forums, professional networking (e.g. Linked-In), and reviews. Most people fall into this category but the true social user will do these things almost exclusively on their various computing devices. This category can utilize the widest list of computing devices closely linked to your living habits. Social users can be broken into two major sub-groups; those that are on the move and those that are not. Those on the move tend to be social in real life and on the go most of the time with those they socialize with. They use computers as tools to stay in sync with a larger gathering of friends and family that they physically see on a regular basis. Those that are not on the move tend to be users that for whatever reason don't have the time or capacity to see others physically and use technology to keep in touch and up to date on what is going on with those they enjoy and miss. The social user can be a very gratifying category, and may consume a large part of your time if not used constructively.

The social user also includes online shoppers. Many of us shop online but the social user tends to be more aggressive towards shopping online and will spend quite a bit of time on sites finding bargains and hard to find items.

Because of the large amount of contacts and the greater financial exposure, this category has become the most sought after category by bad people for financial gain. Security (software and habits) is paramount for this category.

The social user tends to limit their game play to games that come with their computers like solitaire, or free online game site. They tend to not use their computers for running a business or working from home (with the exception of professional bloggers and reviewers). Social users tend to have a limited need for online entertainment but may use social media sites like YouTube.

The Gamer

This category is not for those that simply enjoy solitaire! This is for the people that really want an escape from reality. Many people will not fall into this category at first but may find that this is exactly what they have become. Believe me, I have seen gamers well over their 50s and this is by far the most hard core of all categories. Today's games cover a wide range and are so visually stunning you can find yourself satisfied just spectating as if you're watching a true live sporting event or movie. This can be the most expensive category, especially if you figure out that this is who you are, after you purchase a computer. Before you purchase a computer, you must know that you are a gamer, if you wish to save any money. The only other option to saving money in this category is to learn how to do your own upgrades which is beyond the scope of this book.

A gamer tends to enjoy escaping the reality of the day. It's not limited to obese teenagers playing in dark rooms with pop-tarts and soda. Many professionals enjoy and even need this as a tool to unwind after a stressful day. Others enjoy being able to forget the day to day issues. As stressful as a game can seem, they tend to help a lot of people change their focus, which for them can be therapeutic. Don't get me wrong, there are dangers to becoming so involved with games of this type. A person can forget their obligations to themselves and others. But there is a vast number of gamers that have their virtual and real lives well under control and these are the ones I'm focusing on. You may not know if your prone to being a gamer so here are some things to think about. If you often find yourself wishing you could just stop thinking about certain issues, you may become a gamer. If you have other friends that talk about games, you may become a gamer. If you often find yourself being hyper focused on certain tasks, then you may fall into this category. If you have been curious about certain commercials for games, then this may be a category to look at.

Because of the high level of requirements that your computer must have in order to play some of these games, this category tends to get you computers powerful enough for any other category. But understand that other categories will require software that will not be included in Gaming PCs and for that reason it is not the "cure-all" for what you need to get (despite what others will say).

The SOHO User

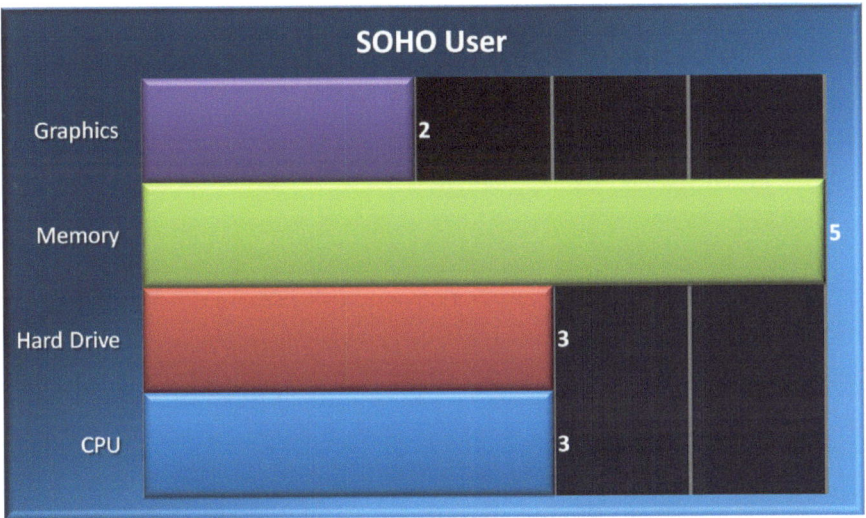

The Small Office/Home Office user (or SOHO for short) is a bit more focused than the other categories. People in this category will tend to have specific software needs and will benefit in knowing they are in the category by purchasing as much of the software in OEM form (described later in this book) during the initial purchase of their computer. SOHO users may have a small start=up business they want to run, a hobby that they want to pursue making money from, or a need to do work from home on a regular basis. There are two major sub-groups in this category: Operators and Management. The big thing with this category is that most SOHO users tend to benefit from having a computer used exclusively for this need. These users should expect to have more than one computer in the home as to keep this computer free from corruption.

Operators use their computers to run software that allow their computers to produce a product, either in physical or digital form. Examples of this may be wedding photographers that needs to edit there their pictures and maintain them digitally. Another example may be someone who uses a computer to control an embroidery machine or vinyl printer. Those that use their computers to work from home tend to need software compatible with what they are using in the office at work. This can be very expensive if purchased after buying a new computer.

Managers use their computers for the management function of running a company. Things like invoicing, payroll, timekeeping, and sales leads are all things that a SOHO management user would use a computer for. Again, with using a computer for a home based business, that contains the financial information of your dreams, it will be best to have that computer dedicated to that task only. Please consider having a second computing device like a tablet, netbook, or notebook for everything else.

The Student

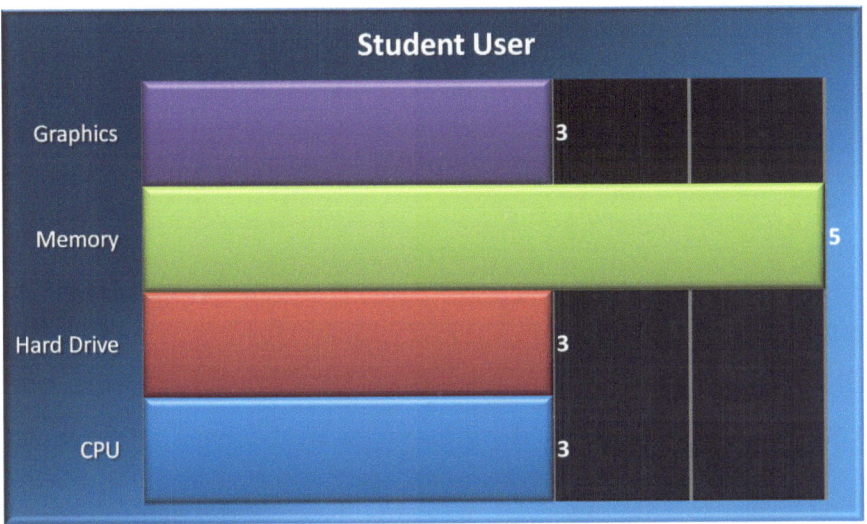

The student category doesn't just refer to people using a computer for homework. This category also includes students that will need to load student versions of professional software to run outside of the classroom. This point is important because users that will be learning things like architecture, graphics design, animation, genetics, and programming will be using software with very high minimum requirements. Some students with the right computers can take their ideas to a reality before they finish school. A great deal of money can be wasted by parents, getting a computing device like a tablet, netbook, or cheap laptop because it seems to be trendy or inexpensive. The problem is that they are great (and fun) as a second computer but not well suited as a student's primary computer. The biggest mistake parents make when buying a computer, for their young adult going to college, is to buy a laptop. After a few months, they find themselves buying a second laptop, because the first one doesn't meet the requirements for the software being studied. Laptops are not very upgradable compared to a desktop, so it's VITAL that you find out what software will be used in advance and get a laptop that meets or exceeds the minimum requirements. If you can't, then you can still save money by buying the strongest computer you can afford. It will cost much less to do this up front and gives you more time to find better discounts. Proactive actions are always less expensive and less stressful than reactive actions!

Because of the nature of a student, these users tend to be more open to, interested, and active in new technology. They tend to relate to every category of this book. Because of this, students will want to place themselves in every category of this book. If you feel that you fall into the student category, please try, as hard as it may seem, to stay focused on this category, especially if you are planning to use this computer in a college setting.

The Entertainment User (Couchers)

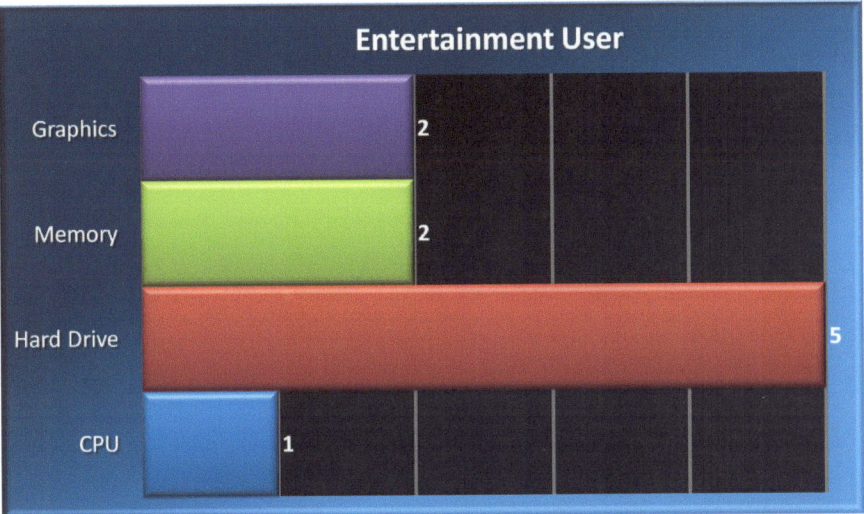

The entertainment user merges computing devices with their home theater systems. This category has evolved, from computers with CD-ROM players, to computers that are fully integrated into all entertainment systems in the home. These computers even have a new name - "Home Theater Personal Computers" or HTPC for short. The Entertainment user wants everything they have for entertainment to be accessible from one location – the couch (hence the term couchers). This is one of the newest and fastest growing categories. The concept behind this category is to have all of your media (songs, movies, videos, and pictures) along with internet access, online movies, games, and communications, centrally accessible to all devices in your home including (most importantly) your primary television. Users here will need to understand, that upgrades down the line are inevitable, and because of this, finding the bottom line, may be a bit harder than it is in other categories.

There are allot of technology devices out there for this category, but I'm focusing on a manageable starting point for getting an HTPC setup. The great thing about this category is that these users are not limited to the type of computing device they use. Other that disk space, most requirements for this category are low. This means that you can even consider replacing a computer you already have with one that better suites who you are, and use your old computer for this category.

What Types of Computers are Out There?

- Workstations
- Desktops
- Nettops
- Streaming Players
- Notebooks and Netbooks
- Tablets
- Smartphones

Workstations

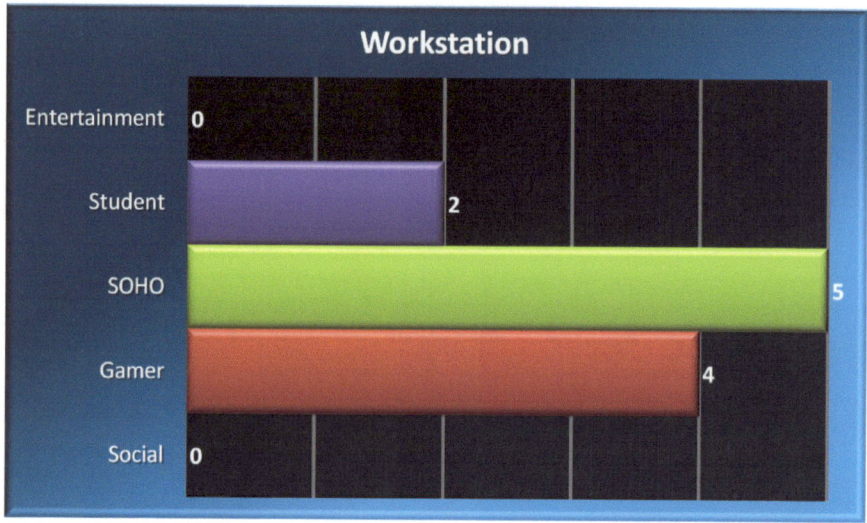

The term workstation has been used often to refer to a company computer, but in the computer world it has a much more specific meaning. These are specialized powerhouses, the biggest and most powerful computers on the market. Workstations come in both Desktop and laptop versions. Workstations are usually used for professional/commercial software with large performance requirements. You'll see computers like these in recording studios, graphics studios, and engineering departments. For the most part you will not need to look at these computers. These computers are best used by SOHO users. Because of their cost, SOHO users tend to be the only users that can get a return on their investment. Gamers would benefit greatly from these computers but the price tends to be a big road block. Most of these computers run 64 bit Operating systems; Max out at over 16 GB of RAM; and support more than one physical, Hi-Speed, multi-threaded, multi-cored CPU. And personally I think they look cool, but that's the nerd coming out in me.

Desktops

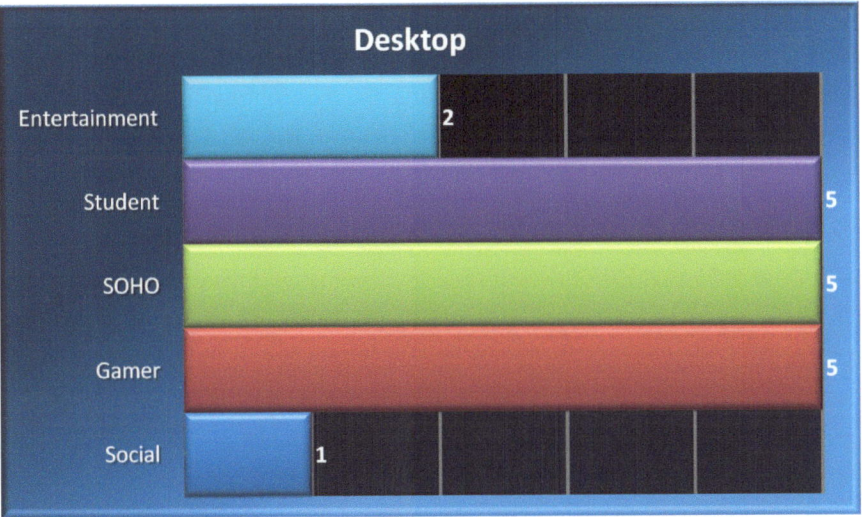

The term desktop in today's technology may be a bit misleading with the vast shapes and sizes of today's computers. But in general, these are the traditional computers you see in the stores that can be placed either on the floor, under a desk, or on top of the desk. Some desktops are integrated into monitors. For the most part, desktops will be the most powerful of any type of computing device you will purchase. The biggest thing to remember is that desktops have the largest capacity for additional high end hardware and the largest range of hardware to choose from. In general, a physically larger desktop can have more additional hardware in it. This is important because, depending on what type of user you are, you may need a desktop to accommodate more than the normal hardware. Desktops tend to work well for students, SOHO users, and most importantly, gamers.

With the advantage of size, the desktop also has the disadvantage of size. For entertainment and social users, the large footprint made by a desktop can be unpleasing to the eye. Many users wanting an HTPC setup will want the computer to be no more noticeable than the cable box or game system. This is where Nettops come into the picture.

Also keep in mind, if you're replacing an old desktop or laptop, these tend to be good candidates for social computing or even entertainment users, with a bit of work. So, if you're a gamer, SOHO, or student, don't throw away your old desktop before considering connecting it to your TV or setting it up in your basement, frog, garage, shed, or spare bedroom as a great way to socialize amongst your friends and family without being forced to do it from your desk.

Nettops

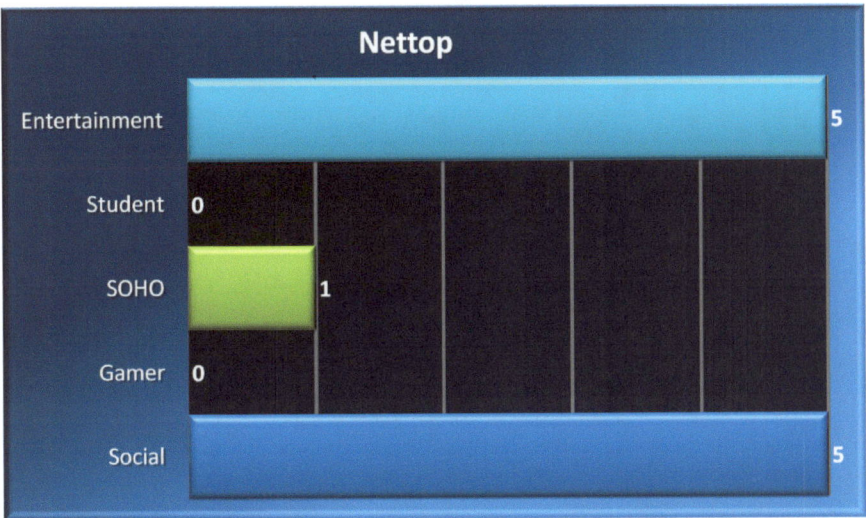

Nettops are fairly new to the market. These are very small computers that tend to work well for entertainment and social users. Do to their size they have limited room for additional hardware and tend to be less powerful overall than the desktops. The good thing is that they tend to be a lot cheaper than a full desktop. Nettops have the benefit of being well suited for small places or for people that want to have a clean looking workspace. Some Nettops can be attached to the back of monitors and many of them have the capability to connect to the internet wirelessly. Another good thing about Nettops is that despite their small size, they **are** actual computers, unlike some of the other devices in this chapter. This means that entertainment users can use these instead of streaming players to gain the full functionality of a computer.

One idea for College students, kids bedrooms, and game rooms is to have one flat screen TV and a nNettop with a wireless keyboard and mouse. This would allow you to use your TV for everything. This works well for a bachelor but may be an inconvenience in a family's den. I personally have this type of setup at my mother's house as a second computer. Her TV is much larger than a computer monitor, so my sister and I use it to show my mother things on the internet that she may not normally be able to see with her poor eye sight.

Streaming Players

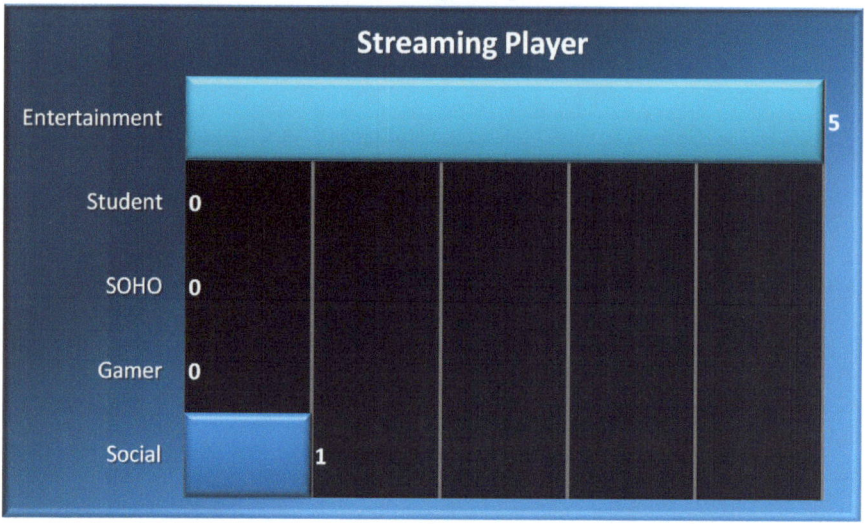

Streaming players are not actually computers in the normal sense, but more of a computing device. Many of them do not have internet browsers and are not capable of running additional mainstream programs although some do give you access to games. These devices have menus with channels (which are basically portals to streaming media web sites like Amazon, Netflix, and Hulu). I figured I would give you the bad part first. So, now for the good parts. Streaming players are designed especially for couchers. They are very small boxes that allow you to access streaming media like music and movies from your TV. They do not require a computer in order to function, only internet access. Unlike gaming consoles, streaming players tend to have a VERY wide range of channels to choose from. They are not very good fits for social users because they have no means to interact with others, although some do give the ability to view things like photos from sites like Facebook. Some have USB connections to connect to things like external drives for greater access to content. Because of the limited functionality of a streaming media player, they tend to be very inexpensive solutions for couchers.

Notebooks and Netbooks

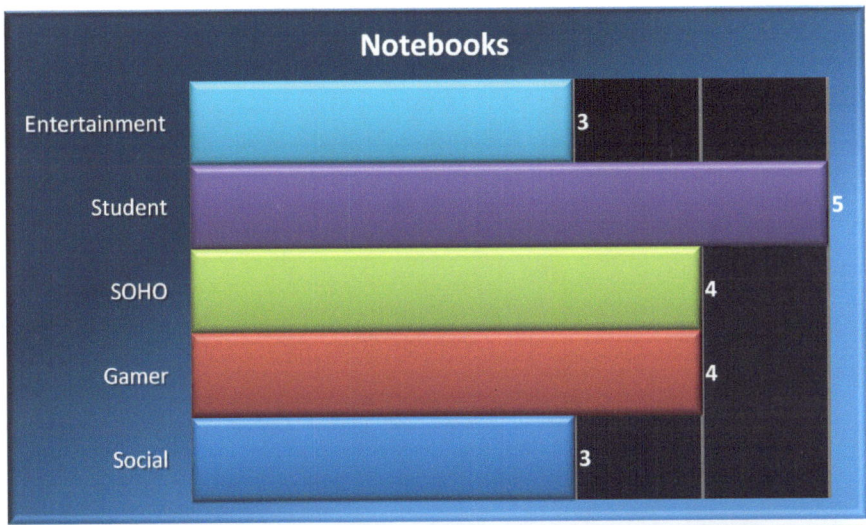

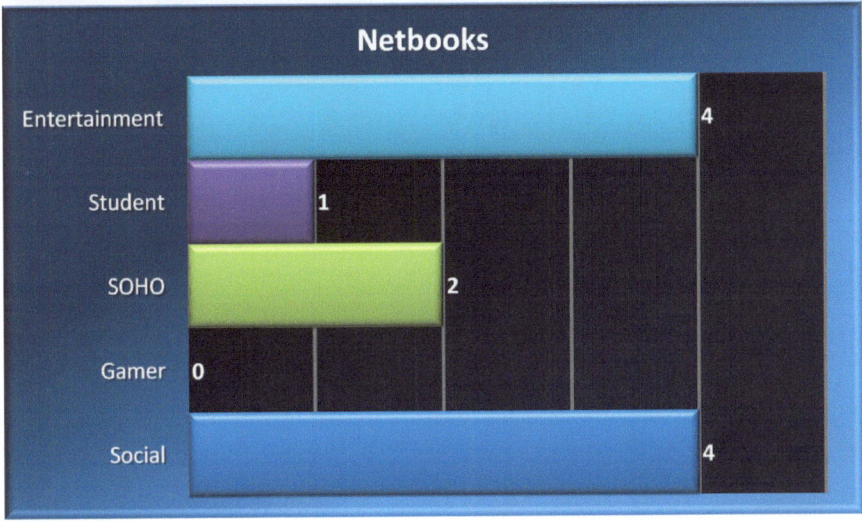

Please understand that there are major differences between Notebooks and Netbooks. They are not the same! Notebooks, from there beginning was designed to be a mobile version of a desktop. Because of this, they can be very powerful and very big (some with screens greater than 19 inches). Netbooks on the other hand tend to be far less powerful with screens less than 11 inches. Both are very portable, but notebooks will have almost everything a desktop has, while netbooks do not include things like CD Drives or memory capacity greater than 4GB (Four

GigaBytes). Students, SOHO, and some gamers will need the power of a desktop with the portability of a nNotebook. Netbooks, due to its size, are well suited for social users as well as great starter computers for teenagers. Keep in mind that nNotebooks and Netbooks do not have much that can be upgraded. Netbooks only tend to have memory and hard drives that can be upgraded. So, it's important to make the right choice on these devices in the beginning, or you may find yourself starting over. Many notebooks and netbooks come with HDMI connections, making them well suited for entertainment users.

Tablets

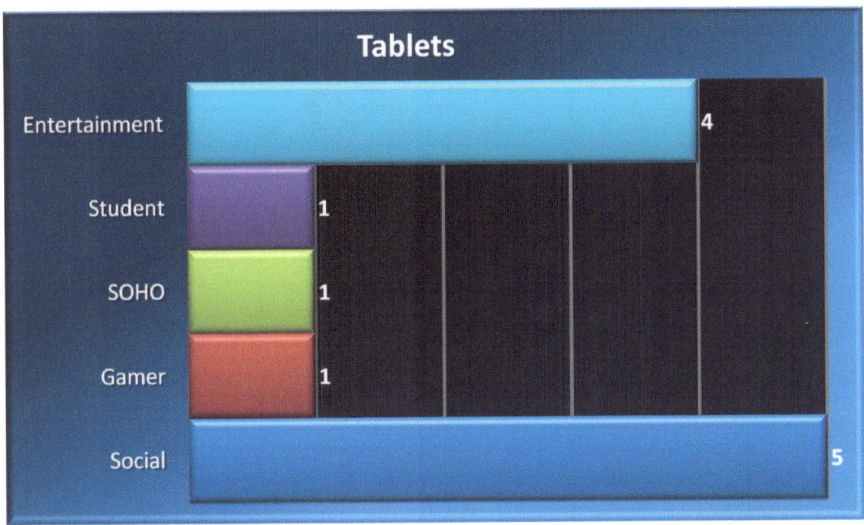

Tablets are very cool devices. They are well suited for the social user, but are also very useful to the entertainment user. They have internet browsers and applications that work very well for social users. Tablets are great for accessing the internet, reading downloaded books, watching streaming video, and listening to music. Some tablets have the ability to use keyboards for working on documents although they tend to not be the best for working on large documents. There is a downside to tablets - tablets tend to have a limited ability to run major applications and are not very compatible with additional hardware. For the most part, what you buy is what you get with Tablets, so SOHO, Gamers, and Students may want to avoid these as their primary computing device. They do, on the other hand, work very well as a second computer for SOHO users. Accessorizing a tablet is limited to a small amount of items compared to a laptop or desktop.

E-Readers fall into this category but not by much. E-readers and tablets are not the same thing. All tablets can be used as e-readers, but only a few e-readers can be considered tables. E-readers like the new Kindle Fire do have the ability to play all forms of multimedia, but they still have limited web browsing abilities, and are limited to only books from one source. E-readers may be well suited for the entertainment user, but only as a secondary device. Social users may be disappointed in their limitations when considering its ability to get social, compared to a tablet. E-readers are great devices and personally I think every house should have one, but they should not be considered a complete fit for any category of user.

Smartphone

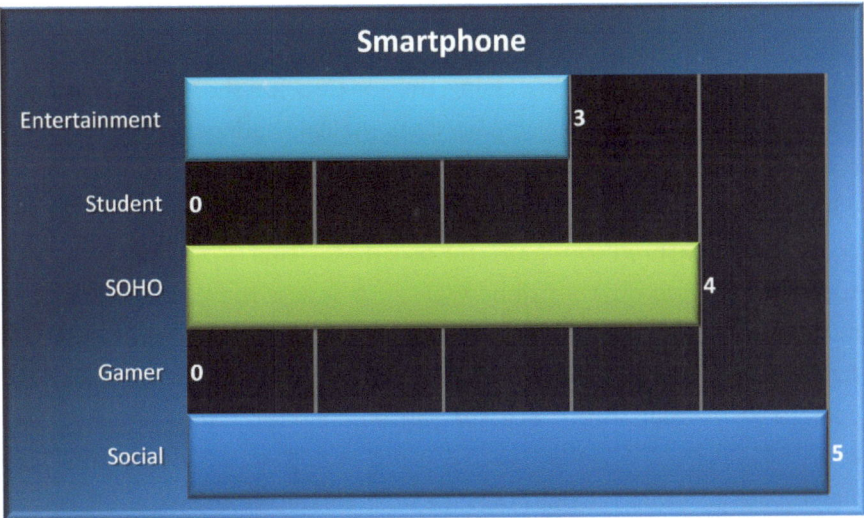

Smartphones are quickly becoming computers in their own right. There aren't many functions a social user can need to do that a smartphone cannot perform; They have just as much capacity to store music and video as a tablet; and by default, have access to the internet from almost anywhere (surpassing many Netbooks, Notebooks, and Tablets on the market in mobility). The main drawback is the small size of the viewing screen and limited availability to accessories like external mice and keyboards. They also tend to have striped down versions of the software that you would see on a desktop. It's important to include smartphones as a computing device because many people already have one. This has to be taken into consideration when your a social or entertainment user because you may find yourself buying something that only adds an additional item to carry with a slightly bigger screen and nothing else. If you do already have a smartphone, then try to learn as much as you can about the features it has. You may find that you already have a pocket sized netbook already. In this case, you would want to look at a less mobile computer device like a desktop, nnettop, or streaming player.

Key Computer Components of a Computer

Processor (CPU)

The processor (cCentral Processing Unit or CPU for short) is the brain of the computer. This is what actually does the calculating when you open a calculator program. It has two main aspects to it that you need to be concerned with - its speed and the number of cores. The speed of the processor (measured in Giga Hertz or GHz for short) is simply the clock speed that the computer can add "2+2". A core is the process of placing more than one processor on the same physical chip (it's the big square thing with a fan on it sitting in the middle of the main board in your computer). A dual core processor can literally add 23453+234534, and add 4345456+423453, then give you the result, at the same time as a single core computer would only be able to calculate 2+2, even if they have the same clock speed. The processor basically gives you the speed that a computer can perform task when you are running programs on it. The faster the processor, the faster it can perform tasks. The more cores it has the more things it can do at the same time. The number of cores far out ways the clock speed. Although software still require a minimum clock speed to operate, the number of cores tend to be a more important factor. In general, cores out ways speed so much that many computers sold today do not even advertise the clock speed, just the number of cores. Most mainstream processors are made by Intel or AMD.

By default every type of user should be looking for at least a dual core processor. Social and entertainment users do not need to be as concerned about CPUs as the others. Gamers need to be looking at the fastest quad core CPUs they can afford. Not doing so will cause them frustration from day one. Games are very hard on CPUs and graphic cards and the performance of fast paced games will be slow and choppy unless they are matched up well. Also many games take full advantage of the technology of the day. More so than any other programs, so having the best performing CPU will be one of two things that must get the lion's share of your money if you are a gamer. **SOHO and students should look first at**

the software they will be using and try make sure the CPU matches or exceeds its minimum requirements.

Hard Drive (HD)

Hard drives are the file cabinets of the computer system. This is where all of your data is stored when the system is turned off. When you open a program the program is read from the hard drive and loaded into memory. The main aspect of a hard drive is its capacity, measured in Giga and Tara Bytes (or GB and TB for short), and how fast they can read and write data to itself (hard drives are based on standards and most conform to Serial ATA (or SATA for short). Think of a hard drive as a file cabinet that automatically retrieves your files and hands them to you. The bigger the cabinet, the more files can be stored in it. The faster it can automatically retrieve the files for you, the faster you can start and finish working. It's almost that simple.

A standard DVD can hold more than 4GB of data for a movie. With that said, and taking any technical specifics away, a 40 GB drive can hold 10 movies. This example is simply to help you understand that the entertainment user (coucher) will want the hard drive to be there primary focuses when looking for a computer. A coucher will want the biggest drive they can get. Also, keep in mind that external drives can be added for storing things like movies and music, but they operate much slower than an internal hard drive. This is because internal drives use SATA technology (at 6 Gbps) to transfer data and external drives use USB technology (at 4.8 Gbps). Believe me, I'm NOT a coucher and I have over 1TB (one TB equals 1000GB with Giga equaling a billion) of movies, songs, and photos on my drive. Gamers will tend to want large drives to accommodate full installations of games to the hard drive. Most of the hard drives being sold today in most desktops and laptops will be well suited for social, Student, and SOHO users so don't be tricked into picking a computer based on the disk space.

Memory

When I explain memory to clients, I use the analogy of a desk. The top of the desk is like a computer's memory. Once you pull the file from the file cabinet, you place the file on the desk. With that said, the larger the desk, the more I can work on at the same time and the larger the file I can work with. As you can imagine, one of the main aspects of memory is size measured in GB. Most personal computers max out at 4GB and other high end systems max out at 16GB. Another important aspect to memory is speed. When a program is opened, it loads into memory. So, the faster the memory the faster the program can function.

Let's say you had a simple program like a calculator program; the program sits on the hard drive until you open it. When you open it, the program then loads into the memory. When you type 4 + 4 =, the question is sent to the processor. The processor then answers the question, but the information to the question comes from and then is sent back to the memory. If the computer is then suddenly shut off, the question, and the answer, is lost, but the original copy of the program remains on the hard drive. In this example the time it takes to send and receive information from memory may not make much of a difference, but with large programs (like for business users or gamers) this can make a huge difference.

Memory is important for student and SOHO users because they tend to work on multiple things at the same time. Having larger amounts of Random Access Memory or RAM for short (same as saying memory) allows you to have more programs open at the same time. It also allows you to work with larger files. Social and Entertainment users will be fine with almost any current systems default amount of RAM. Gamers will want to have as much of the fastest RAM possible due to the size of the games and the performance gain they receive by having the entire game fitting within their RAM. Memory increases the overall performance of the computer, so if you can afford it, try to max it out.

Graphics card

Graphics cards send data from the computer to the monitor. That's the basics of it and for the most part. That's all that a social, entertainment, SOHO, or student user needs to know. Many of today's computers have graphics cards embedded into them that meet any requirement you will need.

Gamers on the other hand, will need to focus hard on this component when making a purchase. Graphics cards use many different methods to convert data into visual images on monitors. Some graphics are generated by the computers CPU then sent to the graphics cards as completed images. The gamer needs to know that in most cases the graphics they see in there games are being entirely generated by their graphics card. For this reason, you can have the fastest computer in the world and still have sluggish game play because of a graphics card that does not meet the games requirements. Graphic cards has its have their own processor called a Graphics Processing Unit or GPU for short. Many computers come with GPUs that are great for the majority of us, and most of them are embedded into the main (or mother) board. A sure way to tell if it's embedded is to look at the back of the computer. There should be a blue or white connector back there. If it's in the same area as the USB ports, then it's embedded. It should be in one of the metal slots near the bottom if it's not embedded. There are exceptions to this, but for the most part, this should be a quick way to tell the difference. A true gamer should never have an embedded graphics card. It's like watching Jurassic Park for the very first time on a 5 inch screen.

What's Current

Processors

There are two main companies that make processors, Intel and AMD.

Intel's has 4 main classes of processors. From top to bottom is as follows:

- 2nd Generation Core i7 Extreme, i7, i5, and i3 Processors
- Pentium
- Celeron
- Atom

Last year's processors are as follows:

- 1st Generation Core i7 Extreme, i7, i5, and i3 Processors
- Core 2 Dou, Quad, and Extreme processors
- Pentium
- Celeron
- Atom

Although the Pentium, Celeron, and Atom may be hard to distinguish, the biggest thing to look for is that any new desktop or Laptop with an "i" processor should have a gold-like broken bar going horizontally thru the middle of it. Most new netbooks, Nettops, and tablets should be dual core. The 2nd generation core i processors have both the CPU and GPU integrated into the same chip to increase performance.

AMD has a lot of different processors so I will summarize them as such. The processors made for laptops are now called APU instead of CPU. They have both the CPU and GPU integrated into the same chip. They also are named by series (from top to bottom A-Series, E-Series, and C-Series). Desktops should have an X2 after or above the designation (for example, Athlon II X2) unless they are simply called Athlon or Sempron (which are both at the bottom of the performance scale).

The processing speed has not changed much over the past year but the increase in the number of cores (with dual core becoming a standard), makes the processor speed a mute issue. Although some new processors have come out this year with single cores, buying a dual core or better will allow you to meet most minimum requirements for your software, and ensure you're getting one of the latest processors out there.

Hard Drives

Hard Drives are pretty standard and the only new things to mention are that they have increased in capacity to as much as 4TB from around 1TB last year. SATA technology has changed. The drives above 1.5 TB are now coming out with SATA 6 Gbit/s instead of the long held standard of SATA 3 Gbit/s. These new drives are literally twice as fast as the older drives. Laptops are still limited to just under 1TB.

Memory

Memory can get a bit confusing so I will keep it simple. The latest RAM is out there is "DDR3 SDRAM". This is literally twice as fast as "DDR2 SDRAM". Try to just remember DDR3. There are many variations of this, based on the clock speed of the RAM, but as long as you are getting DDR3, you can feel comfortable that you're getting a faster product.

Graphics cards

With Graphics cards you basically have two models to know about – Radeon and GForce. These are the manufacturer names of the main processing chips. Most current cards are installed in PCI-e (or PCI Express) slots on the motherboards. The latest is PCI-e 2.0 16x.

Note: (worth mentioning) USB Ports: The latest motherboards now have USB 3.0 ports.

How Computers are Sold

How computers are sold plays a big part in how to save money,. but It alsoit has a lot to do with what you're looking for which is why this comes after the previous two chapters.

Local Store vs. Online Purchasing

Computer manufacturers try very hard to find the best combination orf hard drive, CPU, memory, and graphics for the general user. These configurations are mass produced to keep cost down for both the manufacture and the user. Local stores and online stores purchase and resell these computers, which creates some advantages and disadvantages.

Most manufactures also offer the ability to custom build computers to better fit the user. Manufactures sell these computers at their own online stores. To compete with the manufacturers, most local and online stores offer the ability to perform certain upgrades to preconfigured computers at an additional cost.

Because local and online stores sell preconfigured computers, the computers are immediately available to take home or ship to you. Local stores can offer local in-store warranties. These warranties eliminate the need to speak with the manufactures support department or the need to ship out computers or computer parts. With local in-store warranties, you tend to be able to simply take your computer back to the store and have them fix or replace your device. For this reason, a local purchase can sometimes be the best option to reduce the headache of working with manufacturers that have less than adequate support services. Also, the fact that they have these computers on stock, they can offer deep discount on them when it's time for a new product to be released. The disadvantage to this is that these computers can be sold as new even though they are already out dated. For this reason, it's important to read the "What's Current" section of the previous chapter.

Custom vs. Pre-Configured Builds

The first thing you need to know is the term "Original Equipment Manufacture" or OEM for short. Nearly everything within, loaded, or connected to a new computer has an OEM version of it. OEM simply means something that is sold directly to system builders (manufacturers, local and online stores) for the purpose of selling preinstalled on a computer. These devices or software do not come with the pretty packaging but are still full versions of the same item. Support normally comes from the manufacture that installed it for you and not the company that actually created the device – unless you have it installed in a preconfigured computer by from the store you purchased it from. What's important about OEM parts and software is that they are extremely cheaper than the retail (or BOX) version of the same item. I tell you this because this is where you will save the biggest part chunk of your money. Try to get a computer that comes preconfigured with everything you need. If you're getting a preconfigured computer, get one that does not require having the store upgrade any parts before you receive it. If you need to have upgrades then consider purchasing it online from the manufacture with a custom configuration. Remember, when you upgrade at the store, you are often purchasing what came with the computer and a second addition. Upgrading the hard drive in a store before you receive the computer is like upgrading the tires of a new car before taking it home. The store isn't buying back the tires, so you just bought two sets.

Custom builds are computers that have items added or removed as they are built. They take longer to get, but you only pay for what you want. Custom builds are great for insuring you pay only for what you want. Customizing is ultimately what you want if you are anyone other than a social or entertainment user. SOHO, Student, and Gamers will benefit greatly from custom building their computers.

Pre-configured builds are computers that have been mass produced with the same configurations. They tend to have a lot for less because of this. They are great for social users because they can save a lot of money over custom building your computer. Entertainment users will find this the most common computers purchased by users like them. SOHO users should understand that there is no local store that sells computers tailored for business, so they would be paying for a lot of fluff that they would never use and that fluff would only add to poor computer performance, which in business means money. Students can benefit from pre-configured builds but they need to look closely at what components are installed on it. There are a few computers out there that are specifically designed for gamers. These are called gaming PCs. They tend to cost more than most others. Finding a gaming PC pre-configured will not be too hard and gamers should focus on finding them. Some gaming PCs are designed for specific styles of games, so don't be scared to ask sales staff questions.

Helpful Tools and Cheat Sheets

Matching Computers to Users

Best Computer for Social Users:

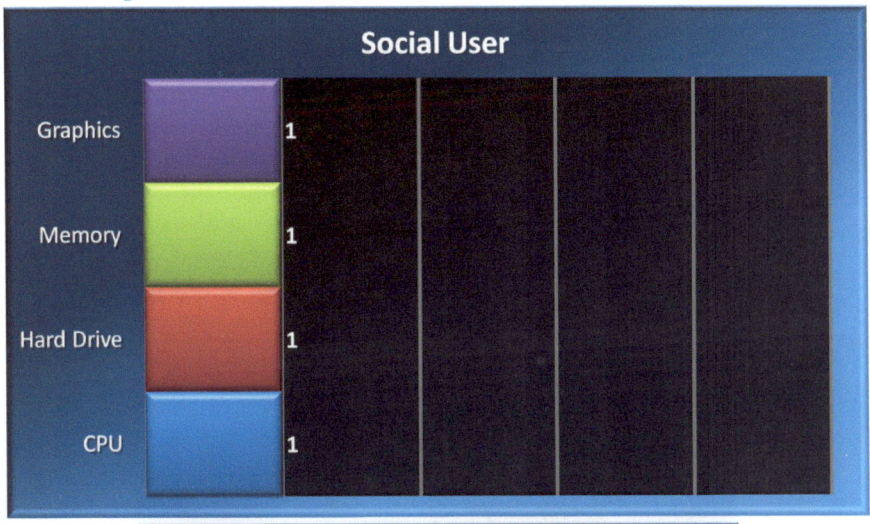

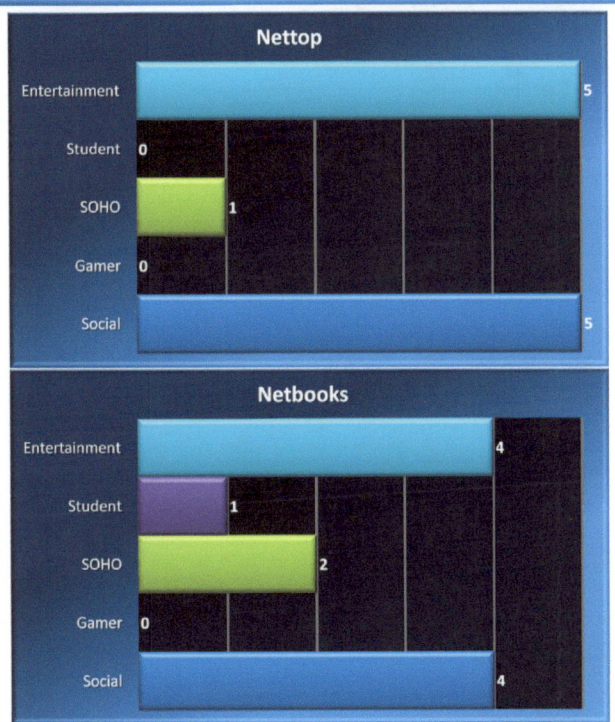

Best Computers for Gamers:

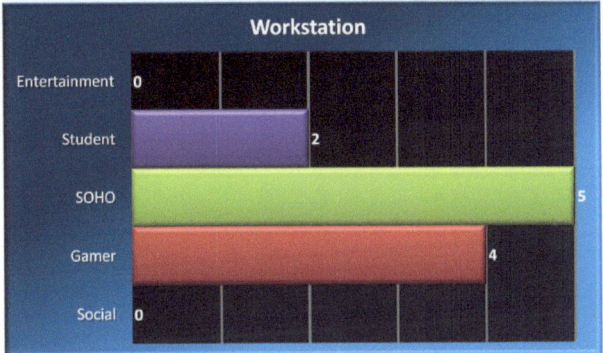

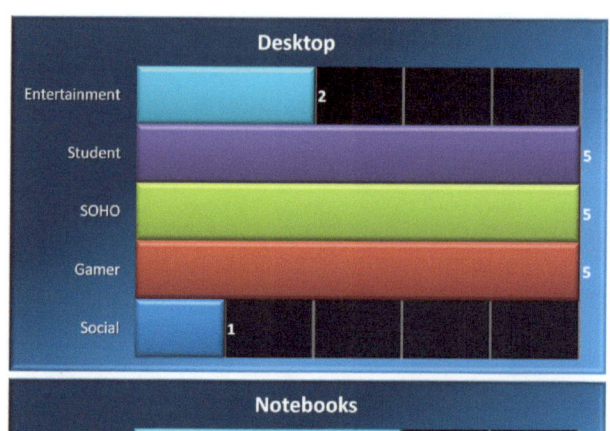

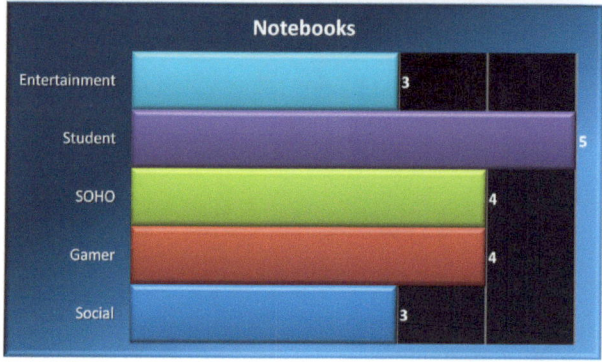

Best Computer for SOHO Users:

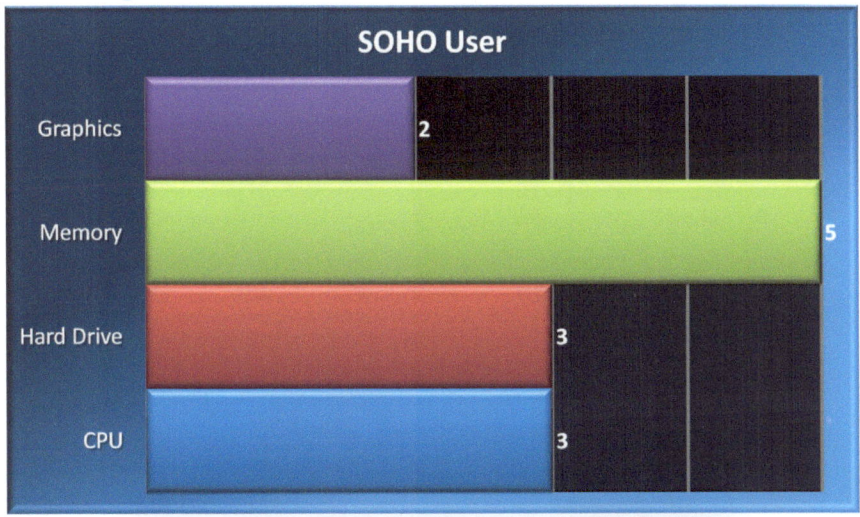

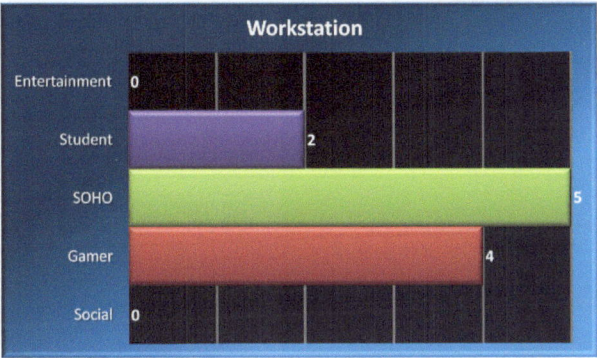

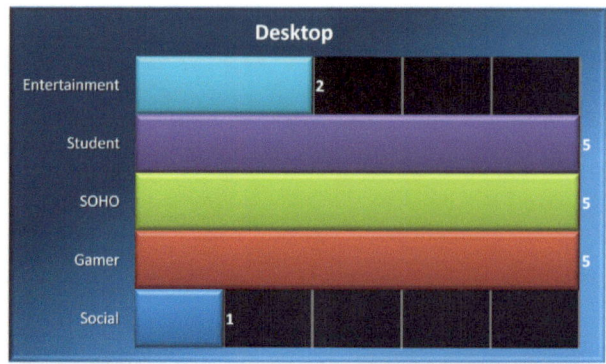

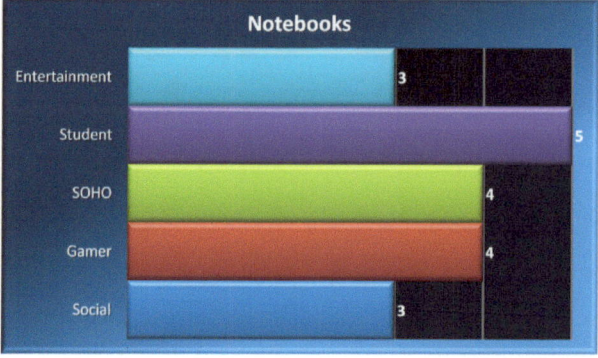

Best Computers for Students:

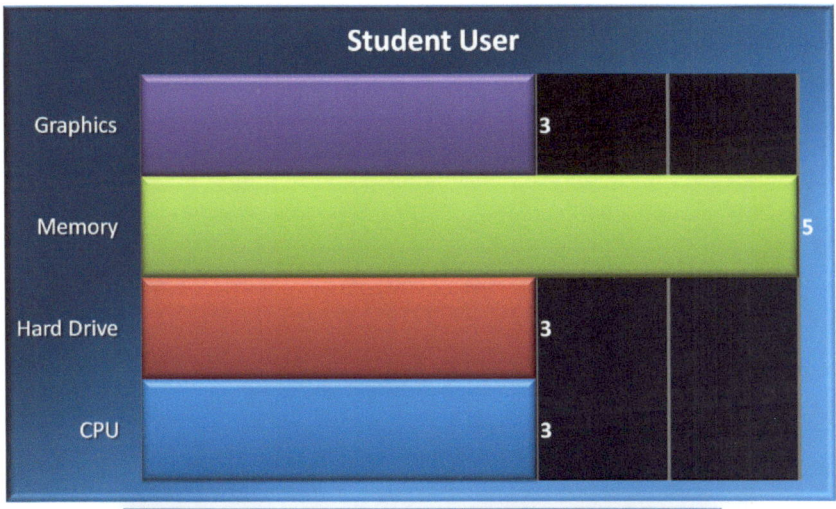

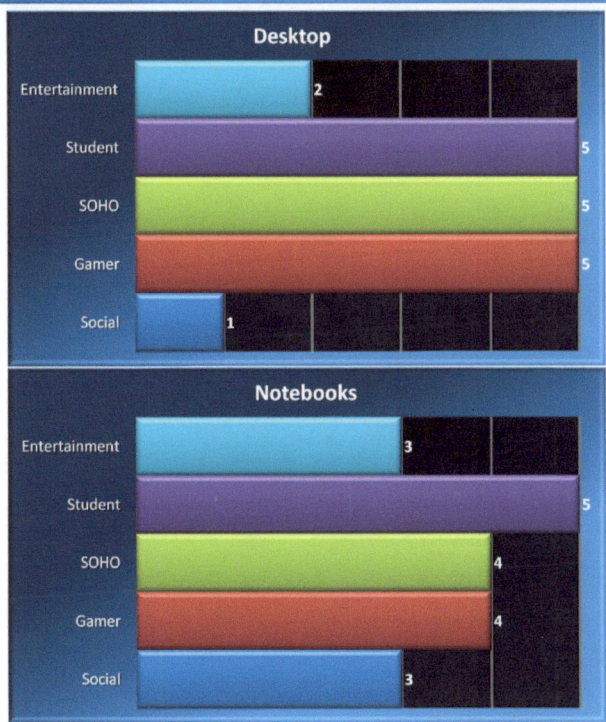

Best Computer for Entertainment Users:

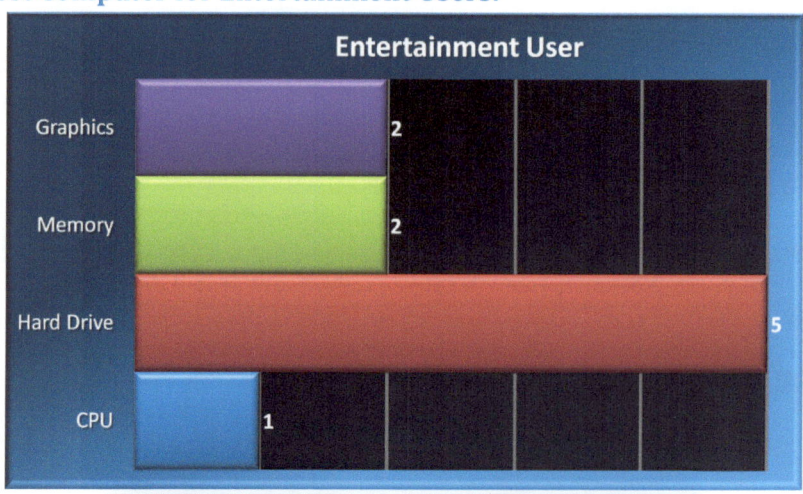

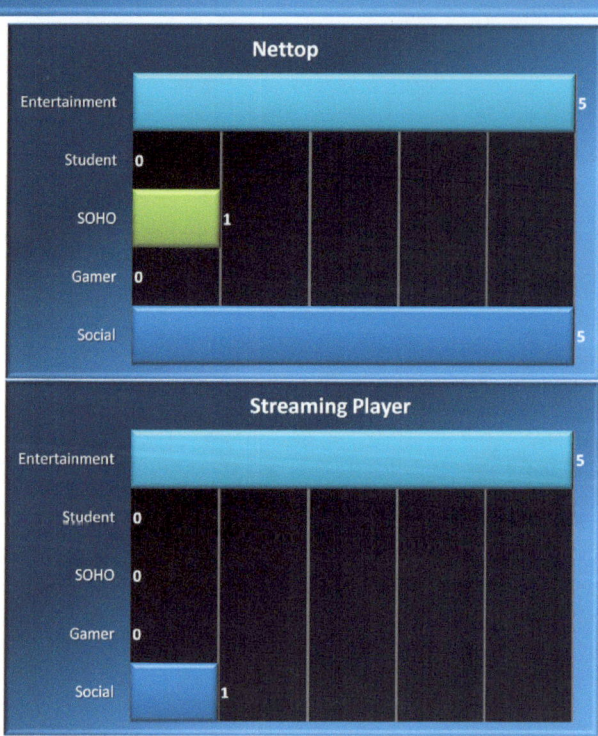

My Computer

Use this form to help you decide what you need. You can take this with you when you go to make a purchase. Show the sales person what you have written down and they should be able to quickly find a computer to match.

Users	CPU	Hard Drive	Memory	Graphics
Social	ANY	ANY	ANY	ANY
Gamer	Best Availible	Greater than 750GB	6GB or Greater	Best Non-Embeded
SOHO	Dual Core 2GHz or Quad Core	Greater than 500GB	8GB or Greater	ANY Embeded
Student	Dual Core 2GHz or Quad Core	Greater than 500GB	8GB or Greater	ANY Embeded
Entertainment	ANY	1TB or Greater	2GB	ANY Embeded

What type of device do I need? _____

What Level of Processor do I need? _____

What size hard drive do I need? _____

How much memory do I need? _____

What type of graphics adapter do I need? _____

What type OEM software do I need? _____

Tips:

- Get the in-store warranty if you're purchasing from a local store. This will save you a lot of time and money in the end.
- Try to find a computer with as much of the hardware you need **preinstalled**.
- Try to find the software you will be using before purchasing a computer, to ensure that the computer will meet its minimum requirements. This will prevent costly upgrades after you purchase your new computer.
- All computers come with the ability to perform an initial backup of the computer for restoring it back to its factory settings. It's very easy to do. Make sure you have a few blank DVDs to go home with your new computer purchase and do it yourself.
- The best source I have found for finding things locally is www.shoplocal.com
- Manufactures tends to have different deals all year long, so be sure to check their sites before purchasing at the store.
- Visit http://200dollar.wordpress.com/ to view my blog, to ask questions about this book's subject matter, downloadable versions of the form in this book, and more.
- Look out for the 2012 and future editions of this book each year for an updated view of the current technology.

Thank you very much for reading my book, and Happy Shopping!

www.ingramcontent.com/pod-product-compliance
Lightning Source LLC
Chambersburg PA
CBHW050831290526
45792CB00001B/344